HOW DO WE PREDICT WEATHER?

by Nancy Dickmann

PEBBLE
a capstone imprint

Pebble is published by Capstone,
1710 Roe Crest Drive, North Mankato, Minnesota 56003
www.capstonepub.com

Library of Congress Cataloging-in-Publication data is available on the Library of Congress website.
ISBN: 978-1-9771-3348-9 (library binding)
ISBN: 978-1-9771-3342-7 (paperback)
ISBN: 978-1-9771-5438-5 (eBook PDF)

Summary: Will tomorrow be cold or warm? Cloudy or sunny? Wet or dry? Meteorologists make predictions about how weather conditions will change. Find out how they do it and what challenges they face in trying to help people prepare for coming weather conditions.

Editorial Credits
Editor: Mandy Robbins; Designer: Dina Her; Media Researcher: Tracy Cummins; Production Specialist: Katy LaVigne

Photo Credits
Getty Images: Joe Raedle/Staff, 11, Universal Images Group, 9; iStockphoto: chee gin tan, 6, tomazl, 26; Science Source: Science Stock Photography, 29; Shutterstock: Aleksandr Vasin, 21, David MG, 27, Elena11, 25,Fineart1, 15, lexaarts, 16, Makhnach_S, design element, Maria Dryfhout, 12, Maria Symchych, 4, Mette Fairgrieve, 13, Nemeziya, 24, NickJulia, 20, Nicku, cover, 1, Sergey Glazunov, 19, Siberian Art, 28, Steven Bourelle, 17, Valentin Valkov, 7, vivanvu, 5, wk1003mike, 10; SuperStock: Dennis MacDonald/age fotostock, 22

TABLE OF CONTENTS

Words in **bold** are in the glossary.

WHAT IS WEATHER?

What kind of day is it? Is the air cold or warm? Is it cloudy or windy? All of these conditions are types of weather.

Weather can change from day to day. In summer, most days are warm. But it might be sunny one day and rainy the next.

Weather can change quickly. A storm might blow in. It changes a hot, dry day into a cool, wet one.

FORECASTING

Scientists study the weather. They **predict** how it will change. This is called **forecasting**.

It's time for school. Do you need an umbrella? Check the forecast!

Lots of people use forecasts. They need to know what the weather will be like. Farmers need rain and sun to help crops grow. Sailors must know when a storm is coming. If you know what kind of weather is coming, you can prepare.

In the Past

Long ago, people had sayings about the weather. Frogs croaking meant it would rain. Spiders spinning meant a dry spell was coming. Some of these sayings had hints of truth. But they were not based on science.

To make a forecast, you must know what weather is like in other places. In the past, people couldn't communicate long distances quickly.

The **telegraph** was invented in the 1830s. It sent messages in minutes. By the 1860s, groups of people used it to make the first weather forecasts.

An 1887 print shows a telegraph operator receiving a message.

Forecasting Today

Today's forecasting is quicker than in the past. Scientists gather weather facts from all over. They check the wind speed. They measure temperature. They track clouds. These facts go into a computer.

A spinning tool can measure how fast the wind is blowing.

The computer looks for patterns.
Maybe there is a big storm at sea.
Where will the wind blow it? The
computer figures out what is likely
to happen next based on past
information.

GATHERING DATA

Meteorologists use many tools to measure weather. They measure it many times each day. Machines take most of these measurements, or readings. Some machines are on land. Others are at sea. They send readings to computers.

floating weather station

weather balloon

Weather can be different high in the air. Scientists send up **weather balloons**. They have tools attached. The tools record the weather in the sky. Then the balloon pops. The tools fall to the ground.

Weather Stations

There are thousands of **weather stations** all over the world. Each one has many tools. Some tools measure temperature. Others measure rainfall. Some measure wind speed. The readings are sent to a main office.

Measurements can be too high or too low if tools are sitting in the sun or the shade. Many weather stations sit in tall white boxes. The boxes have slats to let air flow through them. They help get better readings.

High-Tech Tools

Some weather tools are high tech! Computers are one example. **Satellites** are another. They travel around Earth. Weather satellites take readings from space. They can take pictures of clouds. They show storms moving.

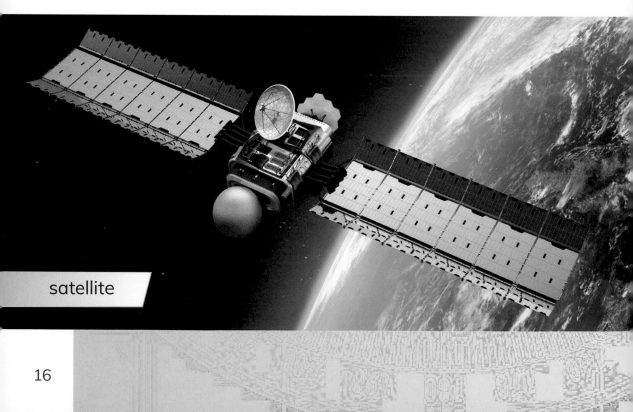

satellite

radar tower

Meteorologists also use a tool called **radar**. It sends out beams of energy. The beams bounce off raindrops in the air. Some beams travel back to the radar. Now it can tell where the raindrop is. It can tell how it is moving.

MOVING AIR

Air feels empty, but it isn't. Air is made up of tiny particles! Each one is very light. But they can add up. A large area of air is heavy. It pushes down on the surface. This is called **air pressure**.

Air pressure is not always the same. It can be high in one area but low in the next. It is lower in high places, such as on mountains. Air naturally moves out of high pressure areas. It moves to low pressure areas.

Air pressure is lower high up in the mountains.

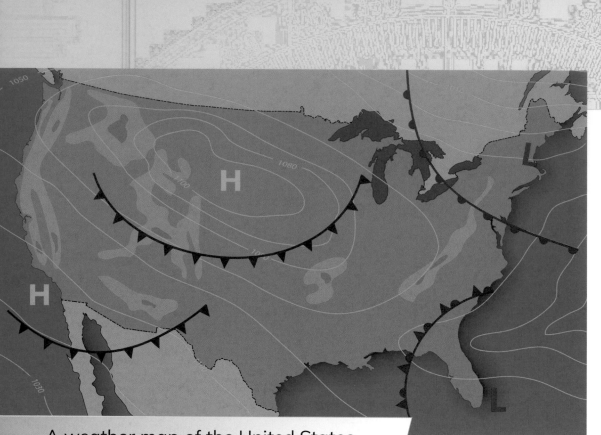

A weather map of the United States shows weather fronts as curved lines.

Tracking Fronts

Air can be warm or cool. It can be wet or dry. Its air pressure can be low or high. A **front** is an invisible line. It separates two different areas of air.

A front is like the front line in a battle. Storms often form along fronts. Meteorologists track fronts as they move. This helps them predict storms. They can also predict weather changes.

A storm front moves in.

PUTTING IT ALL TOGETHER

Weather information comes from satellites. It comes from weather stations. It comes from radar. Computers put it all together.

Computers are good at spotting patterns. Weather in one area might affect the weather in another. Computers can figure this out. They make a forecast. It shows how the weather will change.

The weather is always changing. The farther ahead a forecast looks, the less accurate it can be.

Weather Maps

A map is a good way to show information. Weather maps make it easy to understand forecasts.

Some weather maps are simple. They use symbols to show sun, clouds, and rain. They show temperatures too.

Other maps are more complicated.
They might show fronts and storms.
On TV, the fronts often move over the
map. They show changing weather.

Weather Apps

You can see weather maps in newspapers. They are on TV too. You can also use weather **apps**! They work on phones and tablets.

Apps show what the weather is like now. They also show the forecast. They are updated all the time. If the forecast changes, the app will tell you. Checking an app is very quick. You can do it before you go out.

GETTING IT RIGHT

One app says it will snow tomorrow. Another says it won't. Do you wear your snow boots? Or do you leave them at home? Why are the forecasts different?

The weather changes all the time. A small change in one place can cause a change in another place. Computer programs may **interpret** changes differently. This can make forecasts wrong. Meteorologists are working on ways to make better forecasts.

GLOSSARY

air pressure (AYR PRESH-uhr)—the weight of air on a surface

app (AP)—a program that is downloaded to computers and mobile devices; app is short for application

forecast (FOR-kast)—to predict future changes in the weather; a report of future weather conditions is also called a forecast

front (FRUNT)—the place where one area of air meets another

interpret (in-TUR-prit)—to decide what something means

meteorologist (mee-tee-ur-AWL-uh-jist)—a person who studies and predicts the weather

predict (pri-DIKT)—to make an educated guess about what will happen in the future

radar (RAY-dar)—a tool that uses radio waves to track the location of objects

satellite (SAT-uh-lite)—a spacecraft that circles Earth; satellites gather and send information to Earth

telegraph (TEL-uh-graf)—a machine that uses electrical signals to send messages over long distances

weather balloon (WETH-ur buh-LOON)—a special balloon with tools attached that floats high into the air to measure the weather

weather station (WETH-ur STAY-shuhn)—a box or building with tools for measuring the weather

READ MORE

Hayes, Amy. *Meteorology and Forecasting the Weather*. New York: PowerKids Press, 2018.

Maurer, Daniel D. *Do You Really Want to Drive in a Blizzard?: A Book About Predicting Weather*. Mankato, MN: Riverstream Publishing, 2016.

Sohn, Emily. *Weather and the Water Cycle*. Chicago: Norwood House Press, 2020.

INTERNET SITES

How Meteorology Works
science.howstuffworks.com/nature/climate-weather/storms/meteorology.htm

How Weather Forecasts Are Created
metoffice.gov.uk/weather/learn-about/how-forecasts-are-made

National Weather Service
weather.gov/owlie/

INDEX